365 DAYS

★ ★ ★ ★ ★ ★ ★ OF ★ ★ ★ ★ ★ ★ ★

ROMANCE

Lizzie Cornwall

summersdale

365 DAYS OF ROMANCE

Summersdale Publishers Ltd
46 West Street
Chichester
West Sussex
PO19 1RP
UK

www.summersdale.com

Printed and bound in the Czech Republic

ISBN: 978-1-84953-330-0

Substantial discounts on bulk quantities of Summersdale books are available to corporations, professional associations and other organisations. For details contact Nicky Douglas by telephone: +44 (0) 1243 756902, fax: +44 (0) 1243 786300 or email: nicky@summersdale.com.

To...

From...

JANUARY

Celebrate the start of a new year together by going out for a long walk, especially if it's snowing, and spending the evening curled up under a blanket.

 Bake your favourite cakes or biscuits, and enjoy eating them together in front of a blazing fire.

 On a frosty morning, go out and scrape the ice off your loved one's car windows to save them time and make sure they are safe.

Tell your beloved how much you love something about them that they see as a fault: the way their hair curls, the freckles on their shoulders, the way they say a certain word.

 Kiss your partner five times in a row, perhaps in five different places, and say that's one for each day of this new year together.

 Spend a day shopping for your home – even if you don't live together, treat your partner to that new kitchen gadget or art print they have had their eye on.

Write down one thing you love about them every day in a little notebook and when it is full, wrap it up and give it to them as a gift.

 Give your partner a back massage, just because.

 Agree not to text one another today. Wait. When you get home, talk the night away.

10 Pick out a card that you know they'll like, and give it to them with a special message inside, just to make them smile.

 11 Book a table at your beloved's favourite restaurant as a surprise.

 12 When you're out together, give them your jacket if they are chilly.

Love conquers all things;
let us too surrender
to Love.

Virgil

There is always some madness in love. But there is also always some reason in madness.

Friedrich Nietzsche

Staying in the office late? Call your special someone just to say 'I'm thinking of you'.

 Tell your partner the thing about them that first attracted you.

 Put on some music and slow dance round your living room. It might make you laugh out loud, but you will be laughing together.

On a night when you usually have the evening to yourself, perhaps to go to a class or watch your favourite sport, cancel your plans to spend time with your partner – it will make them feel special.

 Tell them how gorgeous they are first thing in the morning, all ruffled up.

 Kiss your partner goodbye in the morning and be ready with another kiss to welcome them back in the evening.

Tell your partner the ways you feel they make you a better person.

 Change your partner's computer screen saver to show a message of love.

 If they're worrying about their 'to do' list, take note. Next time they're out for an hour or so, do the laundry, fix their bike, sort out the recycling – take that bothersome item off their list.

24 Get your partner a small gift and hide it somewhere in the bedroom. Don't let on until they find it.

 25 If your partner is missing their long-distance friends, arrange for a surprise visit.

 26 Read up on a new way to give your partner pleasure and try it out.

... thou art to me a
delicious torment.

Ralph Waldo Emerson

Of all forms of caution,
caution in love is perhaps
the most fatal to true
happiness.

Bertrand Russell

Play a board game together tonight, and see how much conversation and laughter it sparks.

 Forgive them if they need it. If you know they are feeling bad, be the thing that makes it better.

 Find a nice box for keeping old cinema tickets, programmes from plays you've seen together, romantic notes and other sweet mementos.

FEBRUARY

1 Find an afternoon when you're both off work and announce a movie marathon evening, of your partner's choice.

2 Take a nap together – enjoy the warm feeling of closeness, and how safe and calm your partner makes you feel.

3 Cook a big roast dinner together, complete with pudding, and enjoy the sense of achievement you get to share, not to mention the delicious food!

Laugh at your partner's jokes, even if you have heard them a hundred times! Or better still, tell them some jokes of your own to make them giggle.

 Send your partner quotes from romantic songs, books, films and poems that express how you feel about them.

 Do the washing up on their night, and see their smile light up the room.

Take the time to just listen.

 Give a donation to a charity they believe in.

 Have dinner in Rome or Bangkok – well, set up their favourite takeaway in the living room, put on some music, practise some words and pretend for the evening!

You come to love not by finding the perfect person, but by seeing an imperfect person perfectly.

Sam Keen

Affection is responsible for nine-tenths of whatever solid and durable happiness there is in our lives.

C. S. Lewis

FEBRUARY

 For Pancake Day (the last day before Lent) celebrate by making heart-shaped pancakes for each other, or topping off pancakes with your favourite fillings and feeding them to each other.

 Go outside and build a snowman together, whether it's tiny or huge, and name him.

This Valentine's Day, instead of going to a restaurant for a set menu, plan a date that really reflects your interests as a couple – maybe a pottery class, poetry reading or the theatre; something that you'll both love.

15 Tell your partner the sweet things your friends say about them.

 16 Agree to start a project together. This could range from building a town out of Lego to redecorating the living room, whatever takes your fancy.

 17 Recite a classic love poem to the one you love.

Look at houses together and imagine what your future could be like in your dream home.

 Buy a packet of your partner's favourite sweets. Go through them, taking out their least favourite flavour, and pour the rest into a special container.

 Tell your partner, 'I love being with you, even when we just sit close together and watch TV.'

On your way to meeting your other half, pick up their favourite drink from that cafe they love – it will be a refreshing surprise.

 Notice your partner's favourite TV show or comedian and buy a DVD or tickets to see them perform.

 Watch your other half while they are busy sorting the bills or cooking the dinner, and smile. When they ask 'What?', reply simply, 'You'.

Love reckons
hours for months,
and days for years:
And every little absence
is an age.

John Dryden

'Love' is that condition in which the happiness of another person is essential to your own.

Robert A. Heinlein

Buy your special someone a frivolous present – something they have had their eye on, but know they really shouldn't. You will make their day!

 Get fluffy dressing gowns so you can cuddle up and be cosy together on chilly evenings.

Give your partner a small token for them to wear all day, and say it is to remind them that they are in your heart.

Buck the trend! It's leap day, so, guy or girl, today is the day for that surprise proposal!

MARCH

1 Book tickets to see their favourite musician, and make it a date.

2 Whilst out and about, get your caricatures drawn together for fun.

3 If your partner has lots to do today, catch up on your own jobs – ironing, paperwork, whatever it may be – so that when they are done you will both be free to spend time together, no distractions.

Send some saucy text messages, even if you feel you're 'too old' or too sensible; your other half will always find you sexy.

 Tonight, when your partner is getting ready for bed, lie in their side of the bed so it's lovely and warm for them when they join you.

 Bring home a bar of their favourite chocolate as a treat for the two of you to share.

Love is but the discovery
of ourselves in others,
and the delight in
the recognition.

Alexander Smith

Being deeply loved by someone gives you strength, while loving someone deeply gives you courage.

Lao Tzu

It's been a hard week – how lovely would it be to wake up to breakfast in bed? Make your lover their favourite and bring it to them in bed, be it a full English or simple toast and jam; the thought is what counts.

 If your loved one is performing as a musician, sportsperson or anything in between, be sure to have the widest smile and loudest cheer in the audience.

 Share shower time: enjoy each other's company and imagine you are under a warm waterfall in the tropics.

Plant daffodil bulbs in the shape of a heart in the middle of your garden, and wait for the springtime message to reveal itself.

 Jump in puddles after a rainstorm.

 Today, tell your partner how lucky you feel to be with them.

MARCH

The third Friday in March is World Sleep Day – plan to celebrate by getting to bed nice and early, and see where the night takes you... Just don't forget to get some sleep!

Buy new linen for the bedroom – you'll want to spend even more time wrapped in it than you did before.

Go shopping, and stock up on all your other half's favourite foods. When they open the cupboard, it will be like a hug from you.

Try new food together, even if you consider yourself a fussy eater. Your other half will thank you for taking a chance with them, and you may find something you like!

 Make your partner's packed lunch for them, and leave a sweet message in with their food to brighten their lunch time.

 Go on a walk together and look out for the first signs of spring. You may still need to wrap up warm, but you are bound to see some beautiful sights.

Love grows by giving. The love we give away is the only love we keep. The only way to retain love is to give it away.

Elbert Hubbard

Now here is my secret.
It is very simple. It is only
with one's heart that one
can see clearly.

Antoine de Saint-Exupéry

23 Build a fort in your bedroom for you and your partner to spend the whole day in. Furnish it with pillows, blankets and a duvet.

 24 Take up salsa classes together and learn the dance of passion.

 25 Arrange to meet your partner after work and go for a few drinks. Treat them to every round and compliment them all night, as if it's a date and you're trying to impress them. You will.

Print out and frame some of your loved one's favourite holiday photos.

 Next time they are reading a book, ask them to read some of it aloud, and do the same for them. Include them in that little world you find between the pages.

 Learn to say 'I love you' in three new languages and say it to your partner.

Cut articles or pictures you think your partner will like out of magazines and make a scrapbook out of them to give as a gift.

 Call them when you know they are busy and won't be able to come to the phone; leave a loving voicemail for them to find when they take a break.

 Spend the evening looking after your other half – make their drinks, fluff their cushions, make them snacks – give them all your focus and show them how much you care.

APRIL

It's April Fool's Day – let your lover know you are a fool for them by playing a practical joke on them today.

Tag your partner in some silly pictures on your social networking page – as a cocktail from when the two of you had a night out, as their favourite pair of jeans – whatever will make them laugh!

When two hearts are one, even the king cannot separate them.

Turkish proverb

Romance is everything.

Gertrude Stein

APRIL

 Place a little love note or poem under the driver's-side windshield wiper of your lover's car.

 Have a spontaneous weekend away and explore a new city together.

 Visit a historical house and think about what kind of couple you might have been in the past. Spend time exploring, and walking round the gardens together.

Declare your love to your partner in a very public place.

 Have they had a bad day? Tell them how gorgeous you think they are.

 Dress each other – let your partner pick your outfit for the day, and you can pick theirs. It could be that they have impeccable taste, or you could just end up making each other laugh.

Eat a bowl of saucy spaghetti together, no cutlery allowed.

 Run a bubble bath for two, light some candles and set out some wine and two glasses. Now enjoy the time together.

 Imagine what your dream holiday together would be, if you had all the time in the world.

If you're a gardener, plant your partner's favourite thing, be it peonies or plum tomatoes, so that they can enjoy it when it is grown.

 Take a photograph of something your other half really likes – a cherry tree in blossom, a cat in a shop window – and send it to them, especially if they are having a bad day!

 Sing together in the rain.

17

Life without love is like a tree without blossoms or fruit.

Khalil Gibran

Love is an act of endless forgiveness, a tender look which becomes a habit.

Peter Ustinov

Put a Post-it next to their computer screen as a little, unexpected, note of love.

 Put food or water outside for the birds and watch them together.

 Make extra effort with their parents – help them out in the garden or kitchen. Seeing you together will make your partner even more enamoured of you.

It's Earth Day! Celebrate by having a 'green' date. Eat vegetarian food by candlelight or cycle/take the bus to a talk on sustainability. Whatever you dream up, the Earth will thank you for it, and so will your lover.

Today marks the birthday of the Bard, so celebrate it by reciting some lines from your favourite Shakespeare romance or sonnets to your beloved.

Tell your partner one of the things you love most about them, like the way they laugh, the way they smile, or the way they look when they are sleeping.

 Finished in the bathroom but know your loved one will be in soon? Write them a message on the mirror, either with your finger, or with lipstick.

Find a cafe together and people-watch.

 Join a local gym together and get closer as you get fitter.

 Offer to watch their favourite DVD this evening, even if you have seen it a hundred times.

APRIL

What a happy and holy
fashion it is that those who
love one another should
rest on the same pillow.

Nathaniel Hawthorne

Love is like smiling, it never fades and is contagious.

Paula Dean

MAY

Today is May Day, so find a maypole festival – or dance in the garden together and enjoy the spring air.

 Give your house a good spring clean, top to bottom. It will brighten your partner's day to come into a tidy, fresh-smelling house.

 Stop on your way home and pick up your loved one's favourite dessert for a late-night treat.

MAY

 4 Visit somewhere unusual with your partner that wouldn't normally be considered romantic, e.g. Gnome World. It might be the trip you remember the most fondly!

 5 The first Sunday in May is World Laughter Day. Tickle your lover until they're in peals of laughter... You'll be in fits of giggles too!

 6 Try 'fon-two' – make a fondue dinner just for two – savoury with cheese or sweet with chocolate – and enjoy feeding each other tasty bites.

Feeling brave? Go out on a warm rainy evening and kiss in the rain. Remind yourselves that a kiss can make you forget your surroundings.

 Have you ever brushed your partner's hair, rubbed soothing cream into their shoulders or given them a pedicure? Any of these little gestures will make them feel special and let you get even closer.

 Make a list of things you would like to do but never find the time for, and promise each other that you'll tick off every activity on the list within a year.

Next time you book a weekend away, find somewhere with a hot tub. Wait until the evening to go out and share a bottle of your favourite bubbly under the starry sky.

 How long has it been since you went out dancing? Whether you're a fan of tea dances or late nights clubbing, tonight is the night to take your love out on the town.

 Go out and buy some erotic books – fiction, art or manuals, whatever you choose, look through them together and enjoy the electricity it sparks between you.

Love is like dew that falls on both nettles and lilies.

Swedish proverb

Anyone can be
passionate, but it takes
real lovers to be silly.

Rose Franken

15 If you leave the house in the morning before your partner, let them know what the weather is like to make sure their day goes more smoothly.

 16 Sprinkle some of your favourite perfume onto a light bulb. When the light is switched on, the room will fill with the scent.

 17 Write a romantic acrostic poem using your partner's name, or your special nickname for them.

Choose some essential oils to burn and for massages.

 Be children again – go to the zoo together and hold hands while you watch the monkeys.

 Make a daisy chain for your partner while picnicking in the park.

 Bring home flowers – not for Valentine's, not for a birthday, but just because you are in love.

Tell your partner a secret you have never told anyone else.

 Find a poem, essay or excerpt that you think they will enjoy, and read it together. Not only are you doing something thoughtful for them, you will provoke discussion, which can bring you even closer together.

 Hide love notes in your partner's sock drawer or coat pocket – anywhere where it will give them a lovely surprise.

If the two of you are going out tonight, wear their favourite outfit, the one they say you always look amazing in.

 Massage your partner's hands – it is a small but very intimate thing to do for them.

 Do something you would usually see as a chore together – clear out your wardrobe, go through your old letters or photos – you may be surprised by how much fun you can have doing such everyday things!

A loving heart is the beginning of all knowledge.

Thomas Carlyle

29

Nobody has ever
measured, even poets,
how much a heart
can hold.

Zelda Fitzgerald

Insist your partner plans a special night out with their friends – you can hear all about it when they get back, and enjoy their company even more after some 'me time'.

 Try doing a new adventurous activity together. You could try roller skating, climbing or sailing.

Go out to gorge yourself on delicious strawberries and enjoy the sun together at a pick-your-own farm.

 Set aside a day to cook together. Even if you are not the most competent chef, you can always help with the preparation and washing up.

 Write 'I love you' in fridge magnets and wait for your love to find their surprise message.

And all for love, and nothing for reward.

Edmund Spenser

One can give without
loving, but one cannot
love without giving.

Amy Carmichael

JUNE

 Find out what their favourite scent is and treat them to a few products – candle, shower gel, massage oil – so that they can pamper themselves with it.

 Call your local radio station and broadcast a message of love to your partner.

 Make time for date night – take your love out to one of their favourite places for together time.

 Bake them a cake from scratch. Even if it comes out wrong, it will taste of love.

Go out to the garden together at night and just lie and watch the stars.

 Surprise your partner by doing the jobs around the house they normally do.

 On your way home, collect wild flowers to present to your lover as a bouquet.

 Add some old-fashioned romance into your relationship today – pull out their chair for them, hold open doors, and shelter them with an umbrella if it rains.

JUNE

14 Go for a night of karaoke with your partner and mutual friends. Before you burst into song, dedicate what you are going to sing to your love.

15 Go for a long drive with your partner with no particular destination in mind.

16 Go on a hot air balloon ride together and watch the world go by from up in the clouds.

17 Turn off your phones, the television and your laptops for one entire evening and enjoy just spending time together.

JUNE

 18 Send a postcard in the mail saying: 'I love you for a million reasons, here are the top three...'

 19 Break with routine! If you would normally go out tonight, cuddle up on the sofa. If you would normally stay in, go out for a walk.

 20 Watch the sunset together and reminisce about your first kiss.

The decision to kiss for the first time is the most crucial in any love story.

Emil Ludwig

To love abundantly is to live abundantly, and to love forever is to live forever.

Henry Drummond

A little foot rub can go a long way...

 Book tickets to go to a festival together this summer: music, sunshine and the one you love – what a fantastic combination!

 Write a list of all the things you love about your partner, make it pretty, and put it where you normally put the shopping list. When they read it, it will brighten their day!

Make a creamy dessert like Eton mess, and feed it to each other after dinner, with or without spoons.

 Give your partner a new nickname.

 If you don't have a dog of your own, why not offer to walk someone else's? A perfect reason to go out and enjoy the countryside together.

There is the same difference in a person before and after he is in love, as there is in an unlighted lamp and one that is burning.

Vincent Van Gogh

I want the concentration and the romance, and the worlds all glued together, fused, glowing: have no time to waste any more on prose.

Virginia Woolf

JULY

 1 Send a loving email to your special someone. The unexpected love note will brighten their working day!

2 Breathe in your partner's smell deeply and tell them how much you like it – it will make them smile.

3 Go to see a romantic play together.

If your partner is working on a day that you aren't, meet them from work and walk home with them. They will appreciate you making them a part of your day off.

 Plan a scrumptious picnic on the beach for just the two of you.

Visit your local aquarium and enjoy staring in wonder at the fishes with your arms around your lover.

 Spend a day making sure you touch your partner tenderly.

 Cook a special meal tonight and set up a candlelit dinner for two. When your partner comes through the door, they won't be able to stop smiling!

Write a song to tell your love how awesome you think they are. If writing is not your strong point, change the lyrics to one of their favourites and make it all about them.

 Take some quiet time to sit together and talk about your day.

 Act like you are in an old romance – send your lover a lock of your hair.

12

The little kindnesses
and courtesies are
so important... In
relationships, the little
things are the big things.

Stephen R. Covey

Love and you shall
be loved. All love is
mathematically just, as
much as the two sides of
an algebraic equation.

Ralph Waldo Emerson

Go punting or river-boating together and soak up the scenery.

 Take a run together – it will give you a chance to chat about your day, and you will be getting hot and sweaty and uninhibited together.

 Get a big box delivered to them, with a tiny gift inside.

Ask your partner to name a number between one and thirty, then give them that many kisses.

 Take high tea together – whether you go out to a tea room or make the little cakes and sandwiches yourself, this will be a beautifully old-fashioned romantic treat for the one you love.

 Rent a houseboat for the two of you to holiday in and spend quality time in your cosy nest on the water.

Go to a fairground and kiss on the Ferris wheel.

 Walk barefoot in the grass together.

 If giving flowers, give ones that hold a meaning. Primroses are for first love, peonies for shyness and beauty, and bluebells for everlasting love.

Send a loving text message one word at a time, so they are hanging on your every word...

 Surprise your partner at work with a picnic, or take them out for lunch at their favourite restaurant.

Love is the whole and more than all.

E. E. Cummings

Romance has been
elegantly defined as the
offspring of fiction
and love.

Benjamin Disraeli

Spend the whole day together in the garden – do the weeding, water the vegetables, or just lie in the sun. If you don't have a garden you could spend the day together at the local park.

 Go to a nearby attraction that interests your partner: if they like animals, perhaps a working farm, or if they love wine, a vineyard. Make a day of it.

29 Be creatively nude – paint each other with edible body paint and see where things lead...

 30 Spend some time making yourself look, smell and feel good before they get home, just for them.

 31 Go to your local swimming pool and enjoy the peaceful company of swimming together.

AUGUST

1 Write your partner a love letter, and even if you live together, send it in the post.

2 Bring home a plant that you can nurture together.

3 Serenade your lover. You might not be Sinatra, but you are sure to make them smile, inside and out.

AUGUST

 Go to the races together and bet on your partner's favourite.

 The beach is so much fun during the day, but so romantic at night. Go for a moonlit walk together along the seafront.

Today is World Meditation Day – use this evening to go to a meditation class together, and leave feeling relaxed and centred.

The heart has its reason, which reason does not know.

Blaise Pascal

One does not fall 'in' or 'out' of love. One grows in love.

Leo Buscaglia

Tell your lover, 'I still feel as excited to be with you as I did when we first met.'

 When you know your partner is going to be home late, sprinkle rose petals (or buds of their favourite flower) on the bed and floor around it, light candles around the room, and help them to forget about their day.

 If you are feeling brave, go skinny-dipping together – exhilarating!

Draw or paint your partner. Perhaps you can paint each other's portrait and enjoy the results together.

 Today is International Left-Handers Day – try feeding each other with your left hand only, or writing notes to each other using your left hand.

 Compile a photo album for your partner, packed with memories of times you've spent together, with handwritten captions – a perfect anniversary present!

AUGUST

 Design your own romantic summer cocktails with fruit cut into hearts, or heart-shaped ice cubes.

 Have a spa day – at home or away!

 Arrange a barbecue for your two families and let everyone mingle – a bond between your families will bring you closer together.

Choose henna tattoos for one another.

 If you leave the house before your partner is awake in the morning, leave them a little love note on the pillow.

 Tell your partner what your top ten favourite moments of your relationship have been, and ask what theirs have been.

21

There is no remedy for love but to love more.

Henry David Thoreau

Gravitation cannot be held responsible for people falling in love.

Albert Einstein

Go underwear shopping together and pick an ensemble for each other.

 Give your loved one a book of poetry with the inscription, 'This says it better than I can – I love you.'

 Your mother might have told you never to play with your food, but with your lover, food becomes play… Blindfold your lover and feed them sweet strawberries, creamy chocolate or runny honey.

At the beach, write a romantic message in the sand for you and your partner.

 Take an active interest in your partner's hobby – go along to their book group or yoga class to see what they enjoy and get to know them better.

 Hide a box of champagne truffles in the fridge for your love to find.

AUGUST

 29 Take part in a sporting event and dedicate your participation to your beloved.

 30 Surprise your partner after work – arrive outside their building to meet them and take them on a date.

 31 Find somewhere where you can go on a horse and carriage ride together and enjoy the sights at a leisurely pace.

SEPTEMBER

1 Go for a long hike in the woods – it's a great place for secretive kisses...

2 Take just thirty seconds to stare into your lover's eyes. Think how wonderful it is that this unique human being chooses to spend their life with you, and appreciate all parts of them.

3 Never played strip poker? There's no time like the present! Who knows where it might lead...

So many contradictions, so many contrary movements are true, and can be explained in three words: I love you.

Julie de L'Espinasse

Love is… born with the pleasure of looking at each other, it is fed with the necessity of seeing each other, it is concluded with the impossibility of separation.

José Martí

Call your partner 'lover' all day, and remember that side of them.

 Bake cupcakes and ice them with letters to spell out their name, or a special message.

 Go to the cinema together and pick a film neither of you really wants to see, then ignore it and spend the time kissing in the back row like teenagers.

Find your love a tiny present in their favourite colour.

 Rent out a special vehicle for the day – a stretch limo, a favourite sports car or a convertible – and take it out for a spin together.

 Dance spontaneously together; in the park, the corridor of your building, or just in the street. It will make your partner feel like you are in a scene from a movie.

Today is Mindfulness Day; spend the day being mindful of the way you think and feel about your partner, and the way you act towards them. Let yourself emanate love.

International Chocolate Day is certainly a day for romance – feed each other your favourite chocolates and savour the aphrodisiac.

 Get dressed up for your other half and treat them to dinner, even if it's fish and chips in front of the TV.

Change your alarm to something that will make them smile in the morning – a favourite song or animal noise.

 Plant a tree together.

 Take a shower together and scrub each other's backs.

 Call from the office, just to say 'I love you' – the unexpectedness of it will make it all the sweeter.

We are all born for love...
It is the principle of
existence, and its
only end.

Benjamin Disraeli

The consciousness of loving and being loved brings a warmth and richness to life that nothing else can bring.

Oscar Wilde

If you're out walking, stop to arrange some fallen leaves into a heart or initial, take a photo on your phone and send it to your love.

 Leave little gifts around the house for them: a chocolate on their pillow, a daisy pressed in the book they are reading, a bottle of their favourite bubble bath in the bathroom. Each small gift will feel like a hug from you.

 Get a star named for your lover and present them with the certificate. Tell them, 'You are my star.'

Plan a day off work together and have a mini-holiday in your home town.

 Order flowers to be delivered to your home, so your other half has the added treat of the surprise delivery.

 Talk about how you first met, or first began your romance – remember everything you felt; the nerves, the butterflies... And dig deeper with your partner so you can find out exactly what they were thinking too.

Get your special someone the toy they always wanted as a child but never got.

 Do the housework in a sexy outfit and let them watch.

 Sneak out while your lover is still sleeping and bring home pastries and coffee from their favourite patisserie for a decadent breakfast.

 Go to the cinema and watch *that film*. You know, the one they really want to see, but you don't.

OCTOBER

 Visit a museum together, enjoying the exhibitions and each other's company, and learning something new about the world and each other.

 Go outside and play in the leaves together like kids.

 Tell your partner, 'I love you, just the way you are.'

There is no heaven like mutual love.

George Granville

The anticipation of touch is one of the most potent sensations on earth.

Richard J. Finch

OCTOBER

 Spend the day crafting together – whether you choose to make collages, jewellery or decorative objects for your house, you are spending time together, and you get to enjoy the results as a couple.

 Give your partner a welcome surprise at work – get their favourite sandwich delivered to them, with a little note from you about how tasty they are.

 Write a poem for them; it's something that belongs to no one else.

Make them a mix tape. Put all the songs that remind you of them onto a CD or into a playlist for their MP3 player, and every time they listen to it they will think of you too.

 Take ballroom classes together – it is the dance of romance.

 Plan a weekend away and surprise them, be it Bordeaux or Bognor Regis.

On a rainy day, make it a duvet day
– pull your blanket onto the sofa and
snuggle with the one you love.

 Go to a theme park and hold hands on
the scariest ride.

 Sit on a park bench together and watch
the clouds and the ducks.

Peel a fruit for your partner.

 Go out into the countryside for a twilit stroll together. Look out at the lights of nearby towns and hold hands, taking time to just be together.

 Help your loved one with a new project, with encouragement and whatever back-up you can.

To love deeply in one direction makes us more loving in all others.

Sophie Swetchine

... to love and win is the
best thing, to love and
lose, the next best.

William M. Thackeray

Plan a flash mob dance along with friends to surprise your partner.

Today is Apple Day – celebrate by bobbing for apples together in the garden. See who can get the most, no hands allowed!

 Watch a horror movie together and hold each other for comfort.

Go shopping for items for your home together – make joint decisions so your home reflects both of you.

 Show up early when you've arranged to meet somewhere. Make sure your partner knows you want to spend as much time with them as possible.

 When writing your shopping list, add something sweet like 'kisses' or 'a cuddle from you' in with the everyday items – when your partner reads it they are sure to get a big smile on their face.

Spend the day taking photos of your partner – they are the model and you are the photographer – then make an album of the results. This will be a lot of fun for both of you!

 The park will be quieter now that the days are shorter – sit on the swings together and talk about days gone by.

 On a day of rain and shine, go rainbow-hunting.

Make a little box of some of your partner's favourite things: a shell or rock, a favourite flower, a single chocolate, words from a book – it will be the perfect gift.

 Tell your special someone, 'You make me feel like a nervous teenager – in a good way.'

 For Halloween, dress up as a ghoulish duo, such as Morticia and Gomez Addams.

NOVEMBER

 Go out and collect the prettiest fallen leaves you can find together.

 Buy some balloons and write special messages to each other on them.

 Poach eggs in heart-shaped moulds for breakfast.

NOVEMBER

 Help your partner choose a winter jacket, then they'll stay warm and will know all winter that you think they look great.

Tonight is Bonfire Night – go to your local fireworks display and cuddle against the cold as you 'oooh' and 'aaah' at the beautiful fireworks.

 After a bubble bath you've prepared for your lover, wrap them up in a towel that you've warmed for them.

Love is composed of a single soul inhabiting two bodies.

Aristotle

Each moment of a happy
lover's hour is worth
an age of dull and
common life.

Aphra Behn

Go ice skating together – hold hands to make sure you don't fall!

 Play a game with wishes: ask your partner questions about you or your relationship, and each time they answer correctly, they get a wish from you. See where things lead...

 Treat your sweetheart to the sweetest hot chocolate, topped with marshmallows and cream – perfect for curling up with on a chilly day.

Give your lover a dozen roses but do it with a creative twist: eleven red roses and one white with a note that reads: 'In every bunch there's one who stands out – and that's you'.

 Find a book that your partner has expressed an interest in reading. Take turns in reading a chapter aloud to each other before you go to sleep.

 Surprise your partner by arriving home with a new pair of fluffy winter socks for them.

Indeed, the ideal story is
that of two people who go
into love step by step, with
a fluttered consciousness,
like a pair of children
venturing together into
a dark room.

Robert Louis Stevenson

That is the true season of love, when we believe that we alone can love, that no one could ever have loved so before us, and that no one will love in the same way after us.

Johann Wolfgang von Goethe

Read up on a relaxation technique like reflexology and practise it on your partner; it will bring you closer together both physically and emotionally.

 Order a hamper of goodies from your favourite shop or delicatessen for the two of you to share.

Today is International Men's Day – if your partner is a man, give them extra special treatment. Or, if your partner is a woman, do something special for their father or brother – caring for their family shows how much you care about them.

NOVEMBER

 Save the words 'I love you' for one moment today, and see how much stronger they feel.

 Go on a spontaneous trip to a place that your partner has often talked of visiting.

 Try to recreate your first date together – the place, the outfits, the same food or drink, and remind yourselves of how it all started.

 Hire two old-fashioned bikes with picnic baskets on the front and go on a ride through a park or by a river together.

Collect pinecones together – you'll be able to spray-paint them to make Christmas decorations later, so you can decorate your home with something you have created together.

 Make love vouchers, for example, for a massage or a kiss, and give them to your partner as a playful present.

 Write an alphabet of all the things you love about your lover: a is for adorable, b is for big smile, c is for cuddly etc.

27 Take your partner to their favourite shop and ask them what they like. While their back is turned, pay for the item and give it to them as a gift on the way out.

 28 Tell your other half, 'I fancy you...'

 29 Do your love's least favourite household chore for them and see how much it makes them smile.

 30 Plan a mystery date. Take your partner out and surprise them, making sure they have no idea where you are going together.

DECEMBER

 It's cold and wintry, so warm each other up by cooking the spiciest food of your choice and having a Mexican, Indian or Caribbean day.

 Give your loved one a card that you've adapted just for them. You may have added to the message, drawn extras on, or stuck glitter or cuttings to it. Whatever you do, it will make them feel extra special.

 Make up your own wintry or Christmassy cocktail recipes and try them out together.

DECEMBER

 Hang a pretty heart decoration in your partner's bathroom.

 Make up a story with your partner as the central character. Write it down and show it to them – they are bound to love it, however skilled your writing!

 Take a train somewhere new together – make sure you have goodies for the journey!

 Imagine your lives if you were to win the lottery today: dream about your ideal future together.

8

Never close your lips to those whom you have already opened your heart.

Charles Dickens

Love does not consist in gazing at each other, but in looking together in the same direction.

Antoine de Saint-Exupéry

DECEMBER

 Give your partner an item of your clothing. Whether it is for them to wear, or just to keep, they will always have a piece of you close to them.

 Make sure you buy plenty of mistletoe for your home this winter.

 Write your partner a love letter or poem on one sheet of paper. Glue it to thin cardboard, cut it up into puzzle-shaped pieces and mail each piece to them one day at a time.

 For each of the twelve days of Christmas, from a Partridge in a Pear Tree to Twelve Lords a Leaping, leave a card somewhere your partner will find it.

DECEMBER

 Today, explore your lover's body. If you have been together a long time, you may start to take certain things for granted – look at them again with new eyes.

 Remember, hug.

 If you haven't started your Christmas shopping yet, you'd best begin! Take a trip together and help each other pick out the perfect gifts for friends and family. Make sure you don't let them see you buying their gift, though!

A kiss makes the heart young again and wipes out the years.

Rupert Brooke

… more than kisses,
letters mingle souls.

John Donne

Get a sensual game to play together.

 Instead of giving your partner gadgets they'll never use, give them a weekend away for Christmas, such as to a cabin in a forest: a gift worth cherishing.

 Make a YouTube video of the reasons you love your partner, set to their favourite song.

DECEMBER

 Eat breakfast by candlelight.

 Stop at a photo booth together and keep a small reminder of your loved one with you at all times.

 This Christmas Eve, why not mull your own wine or cider together, and enjoy the results cuddled up on the sofa together, watching your favourite Christmas films.

DECEMBER

It's Christmas Day! Make sure, wherever you are, you get time alone to open your presents, just the two of you.

 Whether you spend Boxing Day with family or friends, enjoy each other's company as you wind down from the excitement and bustle of Christmas.

 Draw smiley faces and pictures on the eggs in the fridge and ask your partner to make you breakfast; wait for their smile when they see your handiwork.

28 While your partner is brushing their teeth at night, leave a hot water bottle under the duvet at the foot of the bed.

 29 Compile a list with your partner of your fondest memories together.

 30 Help your lover conquer a fear; if they are scared of heights, take them somewhere so beautiful they won't notice how high up they are.

In our life there is a single colour, as on an artist's palette, which provides the meaning of life and art. It is the colour of love.

Marc Chagall